A MESSAGE FROM THE PUBLISHER

Hey there, thank you for making the purchase, we really hope you enjoy this coloring experience. If you have the chance, then all feedback is greatly appreciated. We have put a lot of effort into making this book, so if you are not completely satisfied, please email us at support@valentinaesteley.com and we will do our best to address any issues. If you have any suggestions, enquiries or want to send us a selfie with this book, then email at the same address - support@valentinaesteley.com

OUR STORY

Valentina Esteley are a publishing imprint and photography company; specializing in capturing the beauty of our world - for you to enjoy.

Our company focuses on delivering art and photography in print format; principally through stylish coffee table books, as well as empowering a community of photographers and creatives.

 /valentinaesteley

DID YOU ENJOY THIS COLORING EXPERIENCE?

CHECK OUT OUR WHOLE COLORING BOOK RANGE:
valentinaesteley.com/collections/coloring-books

Before You Start

Test your coloring equipment here for bleedthrough. This book has been designed for use with coloring pencils. This coloring book is NOT recommended for paint, pastel or highlighters...

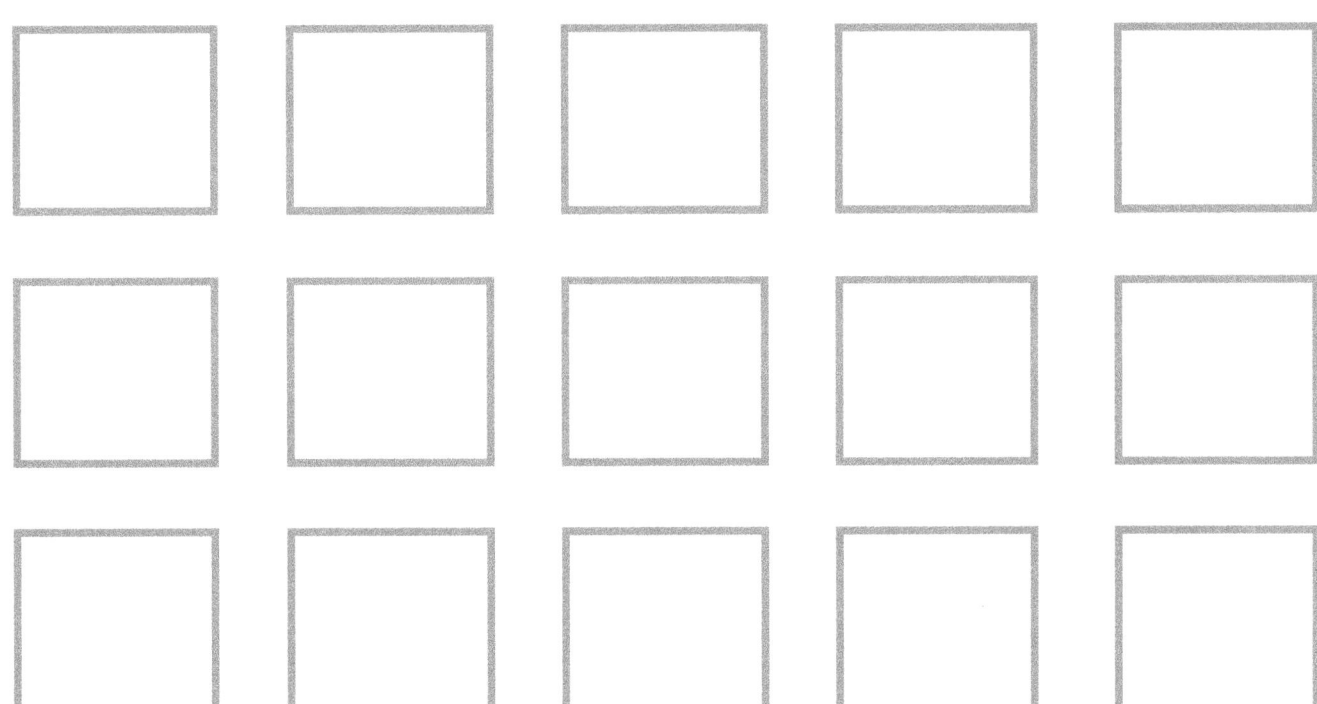

Visit us at www.valentinaesteley.com!

No part of this book may be copied, reproduced or sold without the express permission from the copyright owner.

Copyright Valentina Esteley 2021. All rights reserved.

Ready To Start?

Relax, unwind, and enjoy the experience!

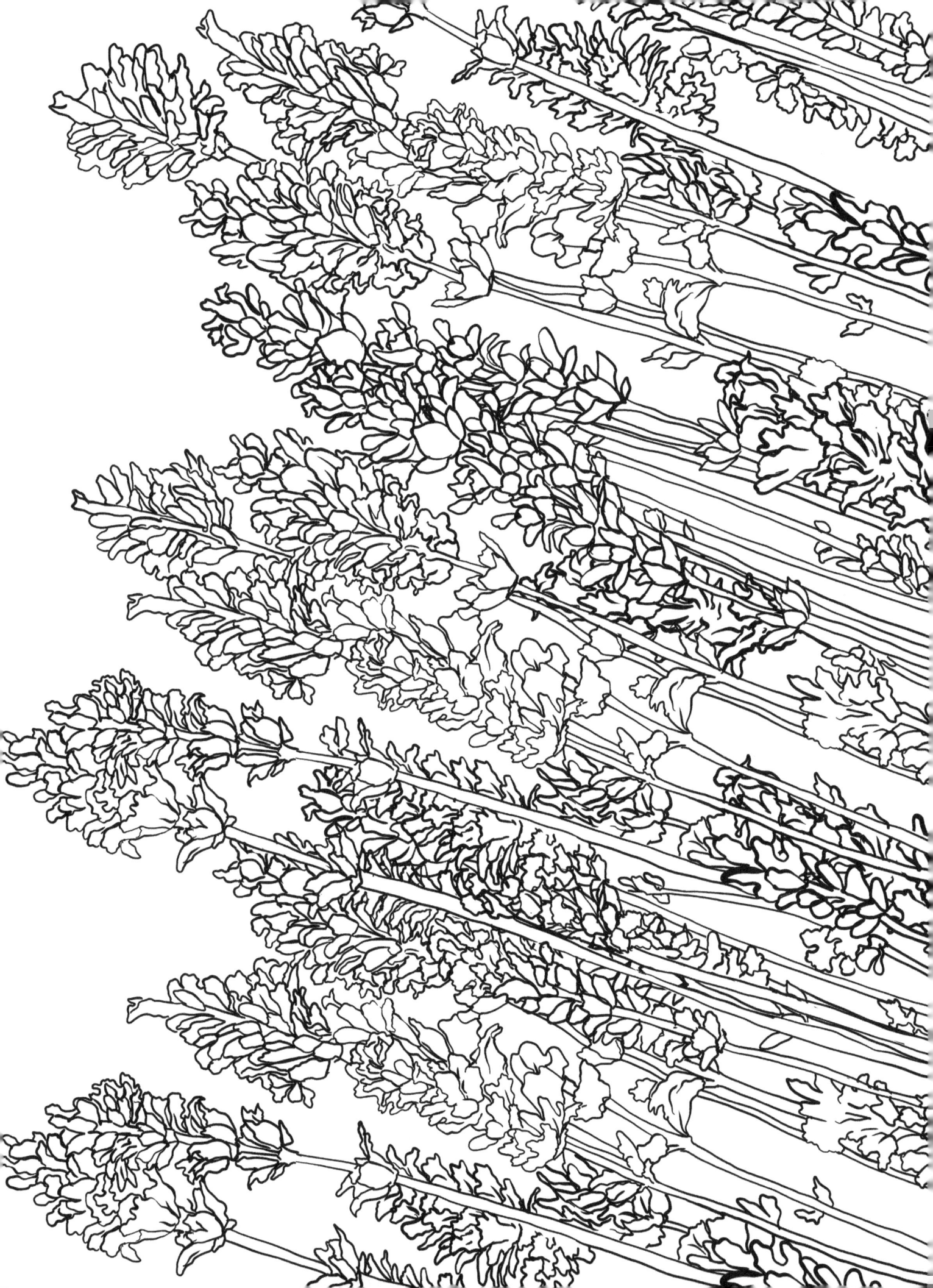

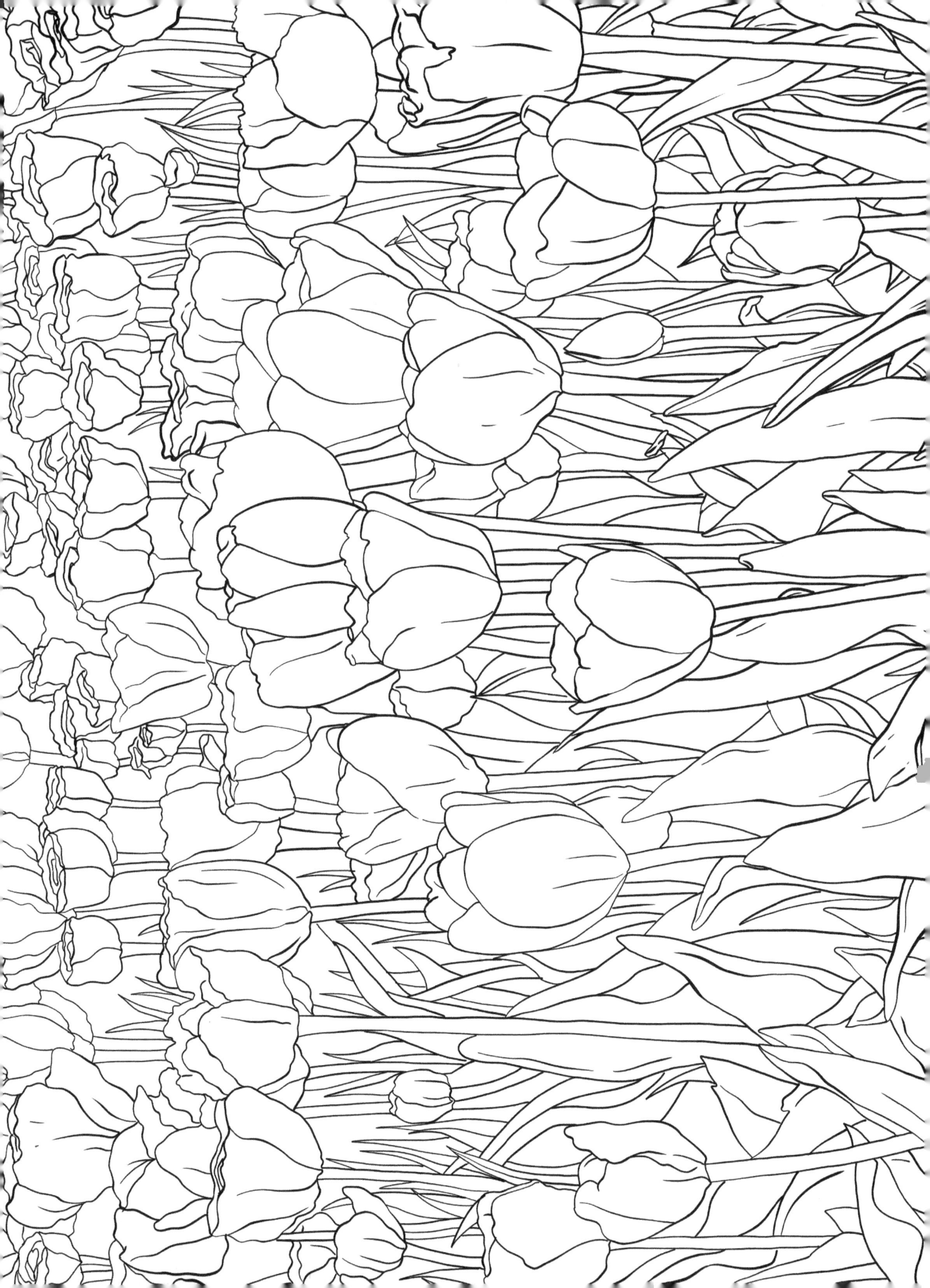

www.ingramcontent.com/pod-product-compliance
Lightning Source LLC
Chambersburg PA
CBHW081455060426

42444CB00037BA/3297